Ela A
275 N
(847) 438-3433
www.eapl.org

P9-DNP-090

31241008026281

MAR 2014

To the children and staff of
Explorer Elementary Charter School
and their wonderfully weedy garden—C. J. E.

For Jim and Beth Fisher,
my favorite farmers—C. F.

BEACH LANE BOOKS • An imprint of Simon & Schuster Children's Publishing Division • 1230 Avenue of the Americas, New York, New York 10020 • Text copyright © 2014 by Cynthia Jenson-Elliott • Illustrations copyright © 2014 by Carolyn Fisher • All rights reserved, including the right of reproduction in whole or in part in any form. • BEACH LANE BOOKS is a trademark of Simon & Schuster, Inc. • For information about special discounts for bulk purchases, please contact Simon & Schuster Special Sales at 1-866-506-1949 or business@simonandschuster.com. • The Simon & Schuster Speakers Bureau can bring authors to your live event. For more information or to book an event, contact the Simon & Schuster Speakers Bureau at 1-866-248-3049 or visit our website at www.simonspeakers.com. • Book design by Carolyn Fisher and Lauren Rille • The text for this book is hand-lettered by Carolyn Fisher. • The illustrations for this book are rendered in mixed media and digital collage. • Manufactured in China • 1113 SCP • First Edition • 10 9 8 7 6 5 4 3 2 1 • Library of Congress Cataloging-in-Publication Data • Jenson-Elliott, Cynthia L. • Weeds find a way / Cynthia Jenson-Elliott ; illustrated by Carolyn Fisher.—1st ed. • p. cm. • ISBN 978-1-4424-1260-6 (hardcover) • ISBN 978-1-4424-4126-2 (eBook) • [1. Weeds—Fiction.] I. Fisher, Carolyn, ill. II. Title. • PZ7.J454We 2013 • [E]—dc23 • 2011018524

WEEDS Find a WAY

Words by Cindy Jenson-Elliott
Pictures by Carolyn Fisher

Beach Lane Books
New York   London   Toronto
Sydney   New Delhi

Weeds find a way to live
where other plants can't grow.

Each weed carries thousands of seeds,
each waiting to make a new weed.

Weeds send their seeds

into the world in wondrous ways:

fluffing up like feathers

and floating away on the wind;

swirled into prickly burrs

that stick to socks and fur,

poking into pants and paws
like tiny needles;

or shot out of tight, dry pods

like confetti from a popped balloon.

Weed seeds find a way to wait,
sitting still in icy earth all winter

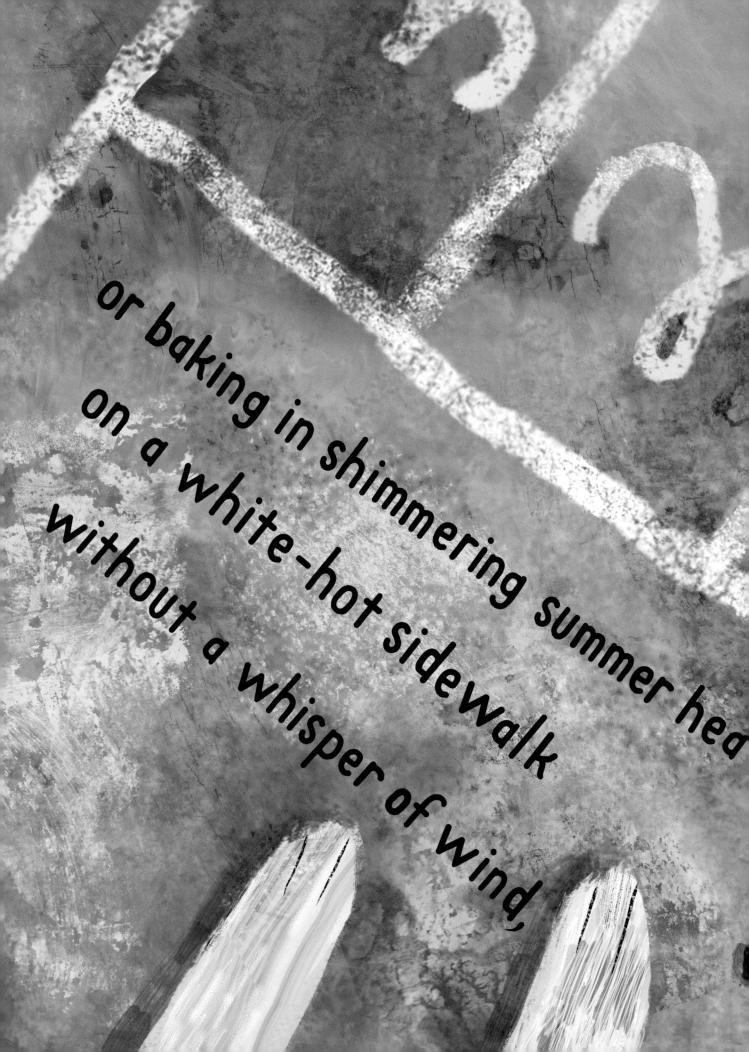

or baking in shimmering summer hea
on a white-hot sidewalk
without a whisper of wind,

till clouds billow,
and soft rain spills,

in the

the

smallest,

stranges

place

they
could
possibly
live.

Weeds find a way to grow:

by the side of a windy road

in a crack in the cellar

of a creaky old house,

in a tangle of tree roots
at the top of a spine of stone,

or wedged in the worn sole of a tattered sneaker.

Weeds find a way to stay,
reaching deep with a grip so strong,
the stem always breaks first,
leaving the living roots behind
to sprout again;

or pinching into pieces

the minute you try to tug them out,

spreading into a spray of plant parts

that find new spots to take root.

Weeds find a way to fight,
hooking tender skin with horny thor
stinging unsuspecting tongue
with invisible prickles,

and surprising hungry insects
with sap so tart,
it could turn a tongue inside out.

Weeds find a way to be loved,
sending up flares of riotous red,
flags of green,
umbrellas of the finest white lace

aking a place sing with bees and birds,
xhaling breath as sweet as sleep.

Weeds find a way to stay—
unexpected guests
who just happen to bring...

the whole family along!

MEET THE WEEDS

Weeds are plants that are often thought to be of no value and that grow in places where people do not want them to grow. By this definition, any plant could be considered a weed if it is growing in a place where someone does not want it to be. But some so-called weeds are actually misunderstood and underappreciated plants that are native to a region and have multiple uses. For example, miner's lettuce (*Claytonia perfoliata*) is native to many areas of North America and has a lovely, delicate flavor. In a farmer's field, however, miner's lettuce is often considered a pest.

Other weeds are invasive plants that have been introduced to a region. Some of these, such as dandelion, purslane, licorice, and horehound, can be used as food or medicine. Many invasive plants migrate around the world as decorative landscaping. If they are well adapted to the climate of a region, however, they can easily escape yards and spread to natural areas. As they spread, these weeds can crowd out native vegetation, block streams, and drive away wild animals. Examples include kudzu from Japan, which grows throughout the South, and the South African Hottentot fig, also called ice plant, which rolls over the coastal canyons of the Southwest like a flat green carpet.

Good or bad, weeds offer endless opportunities to study one of nature's most wonderful tools: adaptation. Adaptations are the physical qualities or behaviors, created by natural selection, that enable a living thing to survive in a particular environment. A weed's adaptations may include physical structures that help the plant avoid being picked, such as a stem that breaks when it is pulled out so the roots are left in the ground to grow, or defenses to prevent the plant from being eaten, such as thorns or poison. Adaptations may also include the way the weed reproduces: by attracting pollinators with color or scent; by scattering seeds via wind, water, or wildlife; or by sending out long underground runners. A weed may also be able to survive on little more than the hope of rain or in the tiniest crack in a concrete world.

Weeds are amazing.

So go outside. Look around. You don't need a garden to know that nature is at work. Chances are, wherever you stand, a weed is nearby, working its way through the soil, finding a way to live and bloom, adapt and grow in tough times and desolate places, making the world more beautiful one blossom at a time.

DANDELION (*Taraxacum officinale*) seeds are not only fun to blow, they are very good for you. In fact, every part of the dandelion is edible. Before they were considered a weed, people all over the world, from the ancient Greeks to the modern day Russians, grew them for food and medicine. Dandelion sap has even been used to make latex rubber. Many people believe that if you make a wish on a dandelion that has gone to seed and blow all the seeds away, the wish will come true.

WILD CARROT (*Daucus carota*) is also known as Queen Anne's lace. It is said to have gotten its nickname when Queen Anne of England visited Denmark and challenged the ladies there to create lace as fine as the flower of the wild carrot.

CRABGRASSES (*Digitaria ischaemum* and *Digitaria sanguinalis*) were among the world's first cultivated grains. Cousins of modern day grains such as wheat and corn, the nutritious seeds of crabgrasses were grown by Stone Age people in Switzerland. Another form of crabgrass, foxtail millet, was grown for food in China around 2700 BC.

MILKWEED (Ascletpiadaceae family) is the host plant for monarch butterflies. These butterflies lay their eggs on the leaves, and the hatching caterpillars eat the leaves. The poisonous sap of the milkweed becomes part of the monarchs' bodies, making them toxic for other animals to eat.

NODDING THISTLE, also known as musk thistle (*Carduus nutans*), was introduced to cool areas of North America and Australia from Europe. In Scotland, prickly thistle blossoms are said to have been scattered on beaches as a weapon against attacking sandal-clad Vikings—ouch!

CANADA THISTLE (*Cirsium arvense*) has invaded twenty-seven crops in thirty-seven countries. Its roots can dive down twenty feet deep.

PIGWEED (*Amaranthus retroflexus*) is a type of amaranth, a grain grown by the Aztec Indians of Mexico as early as the 1400s. Its tiny seeds are high in protein and can be ground into flour or popped like corn.

KOCHIA (*Bassia scoparia*) grows well in the dry, salty soils of the Southwest. It was introduced to the region as cattle forage in ranch lands because it would compete with other more toxic plants.

TEASEL (*Dipsacus fullonum* or *Dipsacus sativus*) has prickly bristles that were used in ancient times as a comb for cleaning wool and for making it more fluffy. Its roots were boiled as a cure for infections. Butterflies and birds are attracted to teasel flowers.

WILD MUSTARD (*Brassica campestris*) has yellow blossoms when it blooms. It is thought to have been brought to North America by Franciscan monks who scattered seeds for the bright blooms along El Camino Real, the road between the California missions, to make the path easier to follow.

STINKWEED, also known as pennycress (*Thlaspi arvense*), has flat, paddle-like seed pods the size of coins. When they are dried, they flutter in the wind, like a plant full of money. Its leaves give off a strong, garlic-like odor when crushed.

OLD-MAN'S BEARD (*Clematis vitalba*) spreads by growing a fluffy "beard" of seeds that fly into the air at the slightest puff of wind. Its vines can grow six feet a year, covering and killing other plants.

SPOTTED KNAPWEED (*Centaurea maculosa*) produces one thousand seeds per plant. Seeds can lie dormant in the ground for five years and then sprout when conditions are right. It eliminates competition by releasing a toxin into the soil to kill neighboring plants.

COMMON BURDOCK (*Arctium minus*) was introduced to North America during colonial times as a medicine, coffee substitute, and fiber for paper. Its burrs are covered with hooks that stick to sheep like Velcro.

COMMON MALLOW and **CHEESEWEED** (*Malva neglecta* and *Malva parviflora*) have been used by Native Americans for centuries as both a food and a medicine. Cheeseweed gets its name from its fruit, which resembles tiny, round, traditional cheeses.

VELVETLEAF (*Abutilon theophrasti*) was introduced from Asia in the 1700s as a possible fiber plant. It thrives by growing taller than any plant around it, stealing the sunshine. Its seeds can stay viable in the soil for as many as fifty years.